Tate the Tattletale Turkey

Written by Lori Kaiser
Illustrated by Lori and Karson Kaiser

Another great book in the Xavier Series!

Visit Lori's website for other great books at:
www.lorikaiser.com

To follow Lori's current writings, visit:
www.kaiserbookblog.wordpress.com

Published by
Fleming Publishing
18204 Cooper Road
Conroe, TX 77302
281-635-2395

www.flemingpublishing.com

© Copyright, 2010 by Fleming Publishing. All Rights Reserved. No portion of this book may be reproduced, stored in a retrieval system, or transmitted, in any form or by any means, electronic, mechanical, photocopying, recording, or otherwise without prior written permission from publisher.
Printed in the United States of America
ISBN 978-0-9845761-6-6

To my new nephew, Tate:
Our wonderful gift from God!

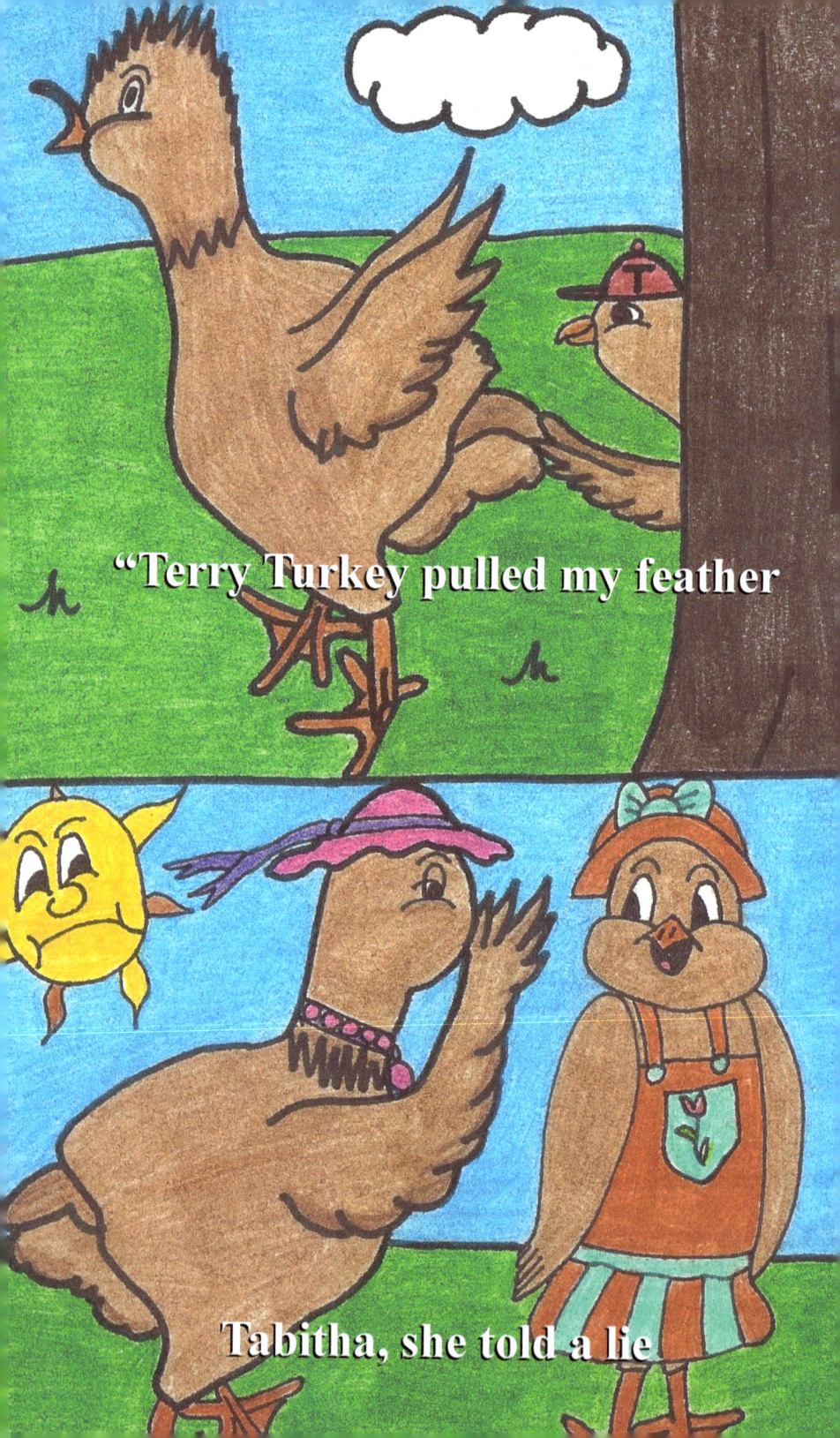

They were on their best behavior
whenever Tate was near;
'Cause he would get them into trouble,
the little turkeys feared.

"Let's go and have a picnic, ask your parents if we can."

Tate soon came to realize that tattling was wrong,

After proving he could keep his word, he gained a slew of friends.

www.ingramcontent.com/pod-product-compliance
Lightning Source LLC
Chambersburg PA
CBHW042046290426
44109CB00001B/50